Vietnamese
cooking MADE EASY

Simple, Flavorful and Quick Meals

by Nongkran Daks, Alexandra Greeley and Wendy Hutton

Your guide to preparing light and flavorful Vietnamese meals at home. This book includes over 50 classic dishes like Fresh Spring Rolls, Hanoi Beef Noodle Soup and Honey Giant Shrimp.

PERIPLUS EDITIONS
Singapore • Hong Kong • Indonesia

Contents

Introduction   3
Basic Vietnamese Ingredients   4
Basic Vietnamese Recipes   8
Appetizers, Salads and Snacks   9
Noodles and Soups   35
Seafood   48
Poultry   65
Meat Dishes   73
Desserts   89
Complete Recipe Listing   96

MAIL ORDER SOURCES

Finding the ingredients for Asian home cooking has become very simple. Most super-markets carry staples such as soy sauce, fresh ginger and lemongrass. Almost every large metropolitan area has Asian markets serving the local population—just check your local business directory. With the Internet, exotic Asian ingredients and cook-ing utensils can be easily found online. The following list is a good starting point of online merchants offering a wide variety of goods and services.

http://www.asiafoods.com
http://www.geocities.com/MadisonAvenue/8074/VarorE.html
http://dmoz.org/Shopping/Food/Ethnic_and_Regional/Asian/
http://templeofthai.com/
http://www.orientalpantry.com/
http://www.zestyfoods.com/
http://www.thaigrocer.com/Merchant/index.htm
http://asianwok.com/
http://pilipinomart.com/
http://www.indiangrocerynet.com/

Famous for its lively, fresh flavors and artfully composed meals, Vietnamese cooking is the true "light cuisine" of Asia. Abundant fresh herbs and greens, delicate soups and stir-fries, and well-seasoned grilled dishes served with rice or noodles are the mainstays of the Vietnamese table. Even the beloved snacks or desserts are often based on fresh fruits served with sweetened rice or tapioca. Rarely does any dish have added fats.

Along with its delicate freshness, Vietnamese cooking is also subtle and sophisticated. Consider the basic dipping sauce *nuoc cham*, which is as commonplace on the Vietnamese family table as salt and pepper are in the West. Made from Vietnamese fish sauce, or *nuoc mam*, plus sugar, chilies, garlic and lime juice, it is at its best when its flavors are balanced between salty, sweet, sour and hot—and this is true of Vietnamese cooking as a whole. Cooks strive for a balance of flavors so no one taste outranks any other. And *nuoc cham* is not the only irresistible sauce that the Vietnamese use, for one of the hallmarks of their cuisine is the generous use of fresh herbs and dipping sauces served on the table to enhance and unify all the flavors of a meal. Another hallmark is the Vietnamese love of wrapping up parts of the meal in rice paper and leafy lettuce, a unique concept for many Westerners accustomed to knife-and-fork eating.

While the cuisine relies on fresh vegetables, subtle seasonings and rice, Vietnamese cooking also reflects strong Chinese and French colonial influences and it has numerous regional differences. In the south, look for plentiful fresh seafood; in the colder north, you'll find slightly heartier meals featuring beef. In central Vietnam, around the ancient royal capital of Hue, the food contains influences of the former court cooks.

But regardless of the region, homestyle Vietnamese cooking calls for an array of simple dishes that make complementary partners at a communal family meal. Dinners customarily call for a soup, followed by a platter of leafy greens accompanied by rice papers and a dipping sauce, seafood or grilled meat or poultry, a vegetable stir-fry, and rice or noodle dish in some form—with hot tea as the preferred beverage. While such meals may look complex to outsiders, most dishes come together easily, although some call for advance preparation to avoid last-minute conflicts. And, as in any type of cooking, planning ahead makes putting together meals much easier.

Modern cooks with well-equipped kitchens and handy appliances will find preparing a Vietnamese meal both rewarding and relatively easy. And with the widespread popularity of Asian foods, locating ingredients is not a challenge—most supermarkets now carry such basics as fresh ginger, lemongrass and chilies, canned or packet coconut milk, bottled fish sauce and dried Asian noodles.

Basic Vietnamese Ingredients

Asian basil   Lemon basil   Holy basil

Basil is often used as a seasoning and garnish in Vietnamese cooking. Several types of basil are used; the most common is **Asian basil** (known as *horapa* in Thailand), which is similar to European sweet basil. It is used liberally as a seasoning and sprigs are often added to platters of fresh, raw vegetables. Similar, yet paler in color, and with a distinctive lemony fragrance, **lemon basil** is used in soups and salads. **Holy basil** has distinctive purple-reddish leaves and a mint-like zesty flavor and is used for stir-fries. Lemon basil and holy basil are not widely found outside Asia. European sweet basil can be used as a substitute for all varieties.

Dried red chilies

Fresh red chilies

Bird's-eye chilies

Chilies have become an essential culinary item in almost every Asian country. Many different varieties are used. The Asian finger-length **red chili** is moderately hot. **Dried red chilies** of this variety are ground to make **chili flakes** or **ground red pepper**. Tiny **bird's-eye chilies** are extremely hot. They are also available dried. The seeds are usually removed when chilies are sliced or minced.

Coconut cream and **coconut milk** are used in many Vietnamese desserts. While freshly pressed milk has more flavor, coconut cream and milk are now widely sold in cans and packets that are quick, convenient and tasty. You can add 1 cup of water to 1 cup of canned or packet coconut cream to obtain thick coconut milk, and add 2 cups of water to 1 cup of coconut cream to obtain thin coconut milk. Canned or packet coconut cream or milk comes in varying consistencies depending on the brand, and you will need to try them out and adjust the thickness by adding water as needed. Fresh coconut cream is made by grating the flesh of 1 coconut (this will yield about 4 cups of grated coconut flesh), adding $1/2$ cup water, kneading a few times, then straining with your fist, or with a muslin cloth or cheesecloth. This should yield about $1/2$ cup of coconut cream. Thick coconut milk is obtained by the same method, but the water is doubled to 1 cup and 1 coconut will yield about 1 cup of thick coconut milk. Thin coconut milk is obtained by adding 1 cup of water to the already pressed coconut flesh a second time and straining again, and this should yield 1 cup of thin coconut milk. You may also obtain thin coconut milk by diluting the thick coconut milk with water.

Coriander leaves or **cilantro** are the leaves of the coriander plant and are often referred to as Chinese parsley. In Vietnam, coriander leaves are used almost exclusively as a garnish. Fresh coriander leaves should keep for 5 to 6 days in the refrigerator if you wash and dry the leaves, and store them in a plastic bag. Italian parsley can be used as a substitute, although the flavor is not the same.

Curry powder is a spice blend made from various combinations of ground spices that generally include cumin, coriander seeds, chilies, turmeric, ginger, cinnamon and cloves. Different spice combinations vary in color and flavor. Look for curry powder in the spice section of supermarkets.

Dried rice paper wrappers are paper-thin wrappers made from a batter of rice flour,

water and salt, that are steamed and dried in the sun on bamboo racks, which leaves a crosshatched imprint on the wrappers. Used to wrap a wide variety of spring rolls, dried rice paper wrappers must be moistened before using. Available in many Asian food markets, they will keep for many months if stored in a cool dark place.

Fish sauce is the ubiquitous condiment used in almost every Vietnamese dish, just as salt or soy sauce are used in other cuisines. Made from salted, fermented fish or shrimp, it has a very pungent, salty flavor in its pure form. Fish sauce is often combined with other ingredients such as sugar, garlic and lime juice to make the various dipping sauces known as *nuoc mam cham*. Use sparingly and look for a quality brand for a better flavor. Refrigerate after opening.

Five spice powder is a blend of fragrant cinnamon, star anise, cloves, fennel seeds and Sichuan peppercorns. This reddish-brown powder is popular as a seasoning in Chinese cuisine and some Thai and Vietnamese dishes. Packets of five spice powder are available in Asian food stores. It is generally used in small amounts as it is quite strong. To keep fresh as long as possible, store five spice powder in the refrigerator.

Galangal is a fragrant root belonging to the ginger family that is used in much the same way as ginger. Known as *kha* in Thailand, *laos* in Indonesia and *lengkuas* in Malaysia and Singapore, it adds a distinctive fragrance and flavor to many dishes. Though available dried or as a powder, try to purchase the fresh root, which has a much richer flavor. Fresh galangal should be peeled before using. The young, pinkish galangal is the most tender and imparts the best flavor. Fresh galangal will keep for several months if wrapped in plastic and stored in the freezer.

Hoisin sauce is a sweet, reddish-brown sauce made from soy beans, garlic, peppers and various spices. Commonly used as a table condiment and flavoring in meat, poultry and shellfish dishes, this Chinese sauce is available in bottles and cans in Asian food stores. Canned *hoisin* should be stored in a non-metal airtight container. Bottled *hoisin* will keep indefinitely when refrigerated.

Lemongrass, also known as citronella, is an intensely fragrant stalk used to impart a lemony flavor to many dishes. The thick lower part of the stem nearest the roots is the edible portion. Discard the outer leaves until you reach the inner core, which should be moist and tender. When using the stalk, bruise it before cooking and remove it from the dish after cooking and before serving. Lemongrass is readily available fresh or frozen in well-stocked supermarkets.

Mint leaves, one of the most common Vietnamese herbs, are indispensable in salads. Mint grown in Southeast Asia has a very intense flavor, similar to spearmint, although regular mint leaves may also be used.

Polygonum or Vietnamese mint (*rau ram*) is an important Vietnamese herb—known as *laksa* leaf in Singapore, Malaysia and Australia. It is served with nearly every

Bun noodles

Rice stick noodles

Rice vermicelli

Glass noodles

Noodles made from rice, both fresh and dried, are widely used in Vietnamese cooking. White **rice stick noodles** (*banh pho*) are used in Vietnam's classic breakfast dish, *pho*. **Bun noodles** (fresh or dried) are thick, round rice noodles that double their size and turn very white when cooked. Fine **rice vermicelli** (*banh hoi*) are similar to *bun* noodles, but thinner. **Glass** or **cellophane noodles** (*mien* in the north and *bun tao* in the south) are dried, translucent noodles made from mung bean starch, which are reconstituted by pouring hot water over them.

meal in Vietnam. Highly aromatic, it has a pink stem and pointed, purplish leaves, and is commonly used as a garnish. A combination of mint and coriander leaves (cilantro) makes an acceptable substitute.

Pomelo, the Vietnamese equivalent of grapefruit, is drier and sweeter than the latter, and has a much thicker and tougher rind. It is eaten dipped in a chili mix, or crumbled and served in salads. It is increasingly available in the West. Grapefruit is a good substitute.

Rice flour is made from uncooked rice grains that are ground to a powder. It is used mainly in desserts. Fresh rice flour may be made by soaking rice grains overnight and then grinding it slowly in a blender. Dried rice flour is sold in packets in Asian stores.

Rice vinegar is mild and faintly fragrant, and is the preferred vinegar throughout Southeast Asia. Inexpensive brands from China are readily available in the West (as well as in Southeast Asia). If you buy a Japanese rice vinegar, make sure you do not buy "sushi vinegar" as this has sweet rice wine, sugar and salt added. If you cannot obtain rice vinegar, use distilled white vinegar and reduce the quantity by about a third.

Rice wine is fermented from freshly steamed rice and has a relatively low alcoholic content. Widely used in Asian cooking, it is readily available in bottles in Asian markets. Japanese sake or dry sherry may be used as a substitute.

Star anise is a star-shaped, eight-pointed pod from an evergreen tree grown in northern Vietnam. It has the pungent flavor of aniseed or licorice. Used most often in soups (*pho*, in particular) or other recipes requiring long simmering, star anise is available whole or ground to a powder. If used whole, remove before serving.

Tamarind is a large, brown tree pod with a soft, sour pulp and hard, black seeds inside. Tamarind pulp is rich in vitamin C and has a tangy, acidic taste. It is used as a souring agent throughout the world. It can be bought fresh, dried, or in pulp form, and the pulp is commonly sold in compressed blocks, with the seeds removed. To make tamarind juice, mix 1 tablespoon of the dried tamarind pulp with 2 tablespoons of warm water, then mash well and strain to remove the seeds and fibers.

Turmeric is a bright yellow-orange root from the same family as ginger and galangal, with a more subtle flavor. It is often used in curries and as a coloring agent.

Wild betel leaves are the spicy and highly nutritious leaves of a vine related to the black pepper plant. In Vietnam, the large, round and crinkled leaf is used as a leafy green in soups, as an outer wrapping for spring rolls and beef, and as part of the standard table garnish. Grape leaves are an acceptable substitute.

Wood ear fungus is a favorite ingredient in Vietnamese and Chinese cooking. Having very little flavor, it is added to dishes for its crunchy texture and to make a fine filling. It is sold both fresh and dried. Soak dried wood ear fungus in water until soft before using. Wash well and discard any hard patch that may be growing in the center of the mature fungus.

Crispy Fried Shallots

4 tablespoons oil
6 shallots, thinly sliced

Yields 1/4 cup (50 g)
Preparation time: **5 mins**
Cooking time: **3 mins**

Heat the oil in a wok or skillet over medium heat and stir-fry the shallots for 2 to 3 minutes, until golden brown and crispy. Remove from the pan and drain on paper towels. Keep immediately in a sealed jar to retain crispness.

Fish Sauce Dip (Nuoc Cham)

2 to 3 finger-length chilies, deseeded and sliced
3 cloves garlic
1/4 cup (50 g) sugar
3 tablespoons freshly squeezed lime juice
1 tablespoon vinegar
3 tablespoons fish sauce
1/2 cup (125 ml) water
1/2 teaspoon salt

Grind the chilies and garlic to a coarse paste in a mortar or blender, then combine with all the other ingredients and mix until the sugar is dissolved.

Yields 1 cup (250 ml)
Preparation time: **10 mins**

Roasted Rice Powder

1/2 cup (100 g) uncooked rice grains

Yields 1/3 cup (100 g)
Preparation time: **5 mins**
Cooking time: **10 mins**

Preheat the oven to 250°F (120°C). Bake the rice in the oven, stirring from time to time, until the rice turns light brown. Do not overcook. Alternatively, dry-fry the rice in a skillet over low heat for 10 minutes, stirring continuously, until fragrant and light brown. Grind the roasted rice grains to a powder in a blender. Store in a tightly sealed container for up to several months.

Peanut Dipping Sauce (Nuoc Leo)

3/4 cup (185 ml) water
1/4 cup (60 ml) *hoisin* sauce
1 tablespoon tamarind juice (page 7)
1/2 cup (120 g) crunchy peanut butter

Combine all the ingredients in a bowl and mix until well blended.

Yields 11/2 cups (375 ml)
Preparation time: **5 mins**
Cooking time: **10 mins**

Grilled Lemongrass Chicken Satays

1 lb (500 g) boneless chicken thighs, cubed

12 bamboo skewers, soaked in water for 1 hour before using

1 portion Fish Sauce Dip (page 8)

Marinade

2 stalks lemongrass, thick bottom part only, outer layers discarded, inner part sliced

3 shallots

1 finger-length chili, deseeded and sliced

3 cloves garlic

1 tablespoon oil

1 tablespoon soy sauce

1 tablespoon oyster sauce

2 teaspoons fish sauce

1 tablespoon honey

1 teaspoon sugar

$1/4$ teaspoon salt

1 teaspoon sesame oil

$1/4$ teaspoon freshly ground black pepper

Serves 4

Preparation time: 30 mins
+ 1 hour to marinate

Cooking time: 10 mins

1 Make the Marinade first by grinding the lemongrass, shallots, chili, garlic and oil to a smooth paste in a blender. Add all the other ingredients and mix well.

2 Pour the Marinade over the chicken cubes and mix until well coated. Allow to marinate for at least 1 hour.

3 Prepare the Fish Sauce Dip by following the recipe on the opposite page.

4 Thread the marinated chicken cubes onto the bamboo skewers and grill, a few at a time, on a pan grill or under a preheated broiler using medium heat for about 4 minutes on each side, until cooked.

5 Transfer to a serving platter and serve hot with the Fish Sauce Dip on the side.

Pickled Bean Sprouts and Carrot

This is a perfect accompaniment for dishes such as Fish in Caramel Sauce (page 53), Caramel Chicken Wings (page 72) or Hearty Beef Stew with Vegetables (page 78).

4 cups (7 oz/200 g) bean sprouts, rinsed well, seed coats and tails removed
2 spring onions, cut into lengths
1 small carrot, cut into matchsticks to yield 1 cup

Dressing
$^3/_4$ cup (185 ml) white vinegar
2 tablespoons sugar
1 tablespoon salt
1 cup (250 ml) water

1 Combine all the vegetables in a large bowl and set aside.
2 In a saucepan, bring the Dressing ingredients to a boil over medium heat. Reduce the heat and simmer for 1 to 2 minutes, stirring occasionally, until the sugar is dissolved. Remove and set aside to cool.
3 Pour the cooled Dressing over the vegetables, mix well and allow to marinate for at least 1 hour. Drain before serving.

Serves 4
Preparation time: **10 mins + 1 hour to marinate**
Cooking time: **5 mins**

Green Papaya Salad

A refreshing and unusual salad made with shredded green papaya, it stands alone or takes such additions as cooked shrimp or beef jerky to turn it into a main dish.

1 large ripe tomato, cut into wedges
1 green papaya (1 lb/ 500 g), coarsely grated to yield 3 cups
1 small carrot, coarsely grated to yield 1 cup
2 tablespoons minced mint leaves
Sprigs of mint leaves, to garnish

Dressing
3 tablespoons freshly squeezed lime juice
3 tablespoons fish sauce
1 tablespoon sugar
2 cloves garlic, minced
1 finger-length chili, sliced
2 tablespoons sesame seeds, dry-roasted for about 10 minutes over low heat until browned

Serves 4
Preparation time: **15 mins**

Combine the Dressing ingredients in a large bowl and mix until the sugar is dissolved, then add all the other ingredients (except sprigs of mint leaves) and toss well to combine. Transfer to a serving platter, garnish with the mint leaves and serve immediately.

Classic Pork and Crabmeat Spring Rolls

Everyone loves these crispy Vietnamese spring rolls known as *cha gio* (pronounced "*cha yoh*"). These take a little time to prepare, but are well worth the effort. Look for rice paper wrappers in well-stocked Asian markets.

12 dried rice paper wrappers (see note) (each about 8 in/20 cm in diameter)
Oil for deep-frying
1 portion Fish Sauce Dip (page 8)

Filling
2 oz (50 g) dried glass noodles, soaked in water until soft, drained and cut into lengths
1 egg, beaten
8 oz (250 g) ground pork
1 cup (4 oz/120 g) cooked crabmeat
1 small onion, diced
2 spring onions, minced
1 small carrot, grated to yield 1 cup
2 cups (3$^1/_2$ oz/100 g) bean sprouts, seed coats and tails removed, blanched and drained
$^1/_2$ teaspoon salt
1 tablespoon fish sauce
$^1/_2$ teaspoon freshly ground black pepper

Accompaniments
12 butter lettuce leaves
Sprigs of mint leaves
Sprigs of coriander (cilantro) leaves
1 small cucumber, cut into matchsticks

1 Prepare the Fish Sauce Dip by following the recipe on page 8.
2 Make the Filling by combining all the ingredients in a large bowl and mixing until well blended.
3 To make a roll, briefly dip a rice paper wrapper in a bowl of water until soft. Remove and place on a dry surface, smoothing it with your fingers. Place 2 heaping tablespoons of the Filling along one side of the wrapper. Fold the closest edge of the wrapper over the Filling, then fold in the sides and roll up tightly, pressing to seal. Repeat until all the ingredients are used up.
4 Heat the oil in a wok or saucepan over medium heat until hot. Gently lower the rolls into the oil, a few at a time, and deep-fry for 3 to 5 minutes each, until golden brown and crispy on all sides. Remove and drain on paper towels.
5 Place the deep-fried rolls on a serving platter with the Accompaniments and serve with dipping bowls of the Fish Sauce Dip on the side.

Vietnamese rice paper wrappers *are sold dried in plastic packets of 10 or 20 and are available in speciality shops. Other types of spring roll or wonton wrappers may substitute for rice paper wrappers although most of them are made from wheat flour and eggs, and the taste is therefore quite different.*

Makes 12 rolls
Preparation time: **45 mins**
Cooking time: **20 mins**

Place the Filling onto a wrapper and fold the closest edge of the wrapper over the Filling.

Fold in the sides, then roll up tightly, pressing to seal.

Fold the closer end of the wrapper over the filling, then fold in the sides and roll up once.

Place two halves of the shrimp on the roll and continue to roll the wrapper up tightly.

Fresh Vietnamese Salad Rolls

These rolls are nothing more than a Vietnamese salad wrapped in rice paper wrappers. The aromatic herbs in the rolls lend a refreshing taste. If you are looking for a unique summer picnic dish, these rolls are perfect!

2 cups (500 ml) water
1 spring onion
8 oz (250 g) lean pork
10 oz (300 g) fresh medium shrimp
12 dried rice paper wrappers (each 8 in/20 cm in diameter)
1 small head butter lettuce, leaves washed and separated
1 4-oz (100-g) packet dried rice vermicelli, blanched for 1 to 2 minutes until soft, then rinsed with cold water and drained
1 baby cucumber, quartered and thinly sliced
1 small carrot, grated
1 bunch coriander leaves (cilantro), sliced
1 portion Peanut Dipping Sauce (page 8)

Makes 12 rolls
Preparation time: **30 mins**
Cooking time: **25 mins**

1 Prepare the Peanut Dipping Sauce by following the recipe on page 8.
2 Bring the water and spring onion to a boil over medium heat in a saucepan and poach the pork for 7 to 10 minutes until cooked. Remove and set aside to cool. Slice the pork into thin strips.
3 Bring the same pot of water to a boil again and poach the shrimp for 1 to 2 minutes until pink or just cooked. Remove and plunge into cold water to cool. Peel, devein and halve each shrimp lengthwise. Set aside.
4 To make a spring roll, briefly dip a rice paper wrapper in a bowl of water until soft. Remove and place on a dry surface, smoothing it with your fingers. Place a lettuce leaf onto the wrapper, closer to one edge, and top with some pork strips, rice vermicelli, cucumber and carrot. Fold the closest edge of the wrapper over the filling, then fold in the sides and roll up halfway. Place 2 halves of a shrimp, side by side, along the roll and top with coriander leaves (cilantro), then continue to roll up tightly to complete the folding. Repeat until all the ingredients are used up.
5 Arrange the spring rolls on a serving platter and serve with bowls of Peanut Sauce on the side.

Vietnamese Seared Beef Salad

The name for this light and refreshing dish translates as "shaking beef". Tender fillet steak, marinated with garlic, rice wine, fish sauce, sugar and black pepper is quickly stir-fried and served on watercress tossed with vinegared onion and olive oil (watercress and olive oil were introduced by the French).

1 lb (500 g) tenderloin
  beef steak, cubed
1 medium onion, halved
  and thinly sliced
1 1/2 tablespoons rice
  vinegar or cider vinegar
1 bunch watercress,
  coarse stems removed
1 tablespoon olive oil
1/2 teaspoon salt
1 tablespoon oil

Marinade
4 cloves garlic, minced
2 teaspoons rice wine,
  sherry or sake
2 teaspoons fish sauce
1 teaspoon sugar
1/4 teaspoon freshly
  ground black pepper

1 Combine the Marinade ingredients in a large bowl and mix well. Place the beef in the Marinade and mix until the beef is well coated. Allow to marinate for at least 30 minutes.

2 Combine the sliced onion and vinegar in a bowl. Set aside for 10 minutes, then squeeze the onion to remove the moisture.

3 Combine the onion, watercress, olive oil and salt in a serving platter and toss to mix thoroughly. Set aside.

4 Heat the oil in a wok or skillet over high heat. Stir-fry the marinated beef for 1 to 1 1/2 minutes until the meat is seared outside but is still pink inside. Remove from the pan and spread the beef on top of the vegetables. Serve immediately.

Serves 4
Preparation time: **15 mins + 30 mins to marinate**
Cooking time: **2 mins**

Seasoned Shrimp on a Sugar Cane Stick

This is another classic Vietnamese dish that is totally unique. A stick of sugar cane is used as a skewer and each bite releases a burst of sweet cane juice.

2 tablespoons oil
8 sugar cane sticks (see note), each 6 in/15 cm in length
1 portion Fish Sauce Dip (page 8)

Seasoned Shrimp
1 teaspoon salt
10 oz (300 g) fresh medium shrimp, peeled and deveined
$1/4$ cup (2 oz/50 g) ground chicken
$1/4$ cup (3 oz/80 g) white fish fillet
3 cloves garlic
3 shallots
1 teaspoon sugar
1 egg white, beaten
1 tablespoon fish sauce
1 tablespoon Roasted Rice Powder (page 8)
$1/4$ teaspoon freshly ground black pepper

Garnishes
1 head butter lettuce, leaves washed and separated
3 oz (80 g) dried rice vermicelli, blanched for 1 to 2 minutes until soft, then rinsed with cold water and drained (optional)
Sprigs of coriander leaves (cilantro)
Sprigs of mint leaves

1 Prepare the Fish Sauce Dip by following the recipe on page 8.

2 Make the Seasoned Shrimp by rubbing the salt into the shrimp. Set the shrimp aside for 15 minutes, then rinse and drain. Grind the shrimp, chicken, fish fillet, garlic, shallots and sugar to a paste in a blender, then combine with all the other ingredients and mix until well blended. Divide the Seasoned Shrimp into 8 equal portions.

3 Lightly grease your hands with a little oil, wrap a portion of the Seasoned Shrimp tightly around the middle of a sugar cane stick. Repeat with the remaining ingredients to make a total of 8 sticks.

4 Grill the sugar cane skewers on a pan grill or under a preheated broiler using medium heat for 5 to 10 minutes, turning frequently until slightly browned on all sides. Remove from the heat and place on a serving platter.

5 On individual serving platters, arrange the cooked shrimp sticks on a bed of garnishes made up of lettuce, rice vermicelli (if using), coriander (cilantro) and mint leaves. Serve with dipping bowls of the Fish Sauce Dip on the side. The photo on the right shows an elegant presentation with sticks removed, however, half the fun of eating this dish is chewing on the sugar cane sticks.

*Fresh **sugar cane** looks like bamboo and is available in many Asian and Caribbean markets. It is also sold canned or frozen. When using fresh cane, peel off the outer skin using a knife, then split the cane lengthwise into sticks.*

Serves 4 to 6
Preparation time: **45 mins**
Cooking time: **15 mins**

Grease your hands, wrap the Seasoned Shrimp around the middle of a sugar cane stick.

Grill the shrimp sticks until browned on all sides.

Shredded Chicken and Cabbage Salad

Think of this dish as the Vietnamese version of Chinese chicken salad, a dish of shredded cabbage with chicken and a tangy sweet and sour dressing. But this recipe contains refreshing mint leaves and pungent fish sauce, with a sprinkling of crushed peanuts, turning it into a light yet satisfying meal. You can make the dressing in advance and refrigerate it until ready to use. Plan to serve this dish as part of a whole meal to serve 6; alternatively, this recipe makes a light main dish serving 4.

1 large or 2 small chicken breasts (about 8 oz/ 250 g), poached until cooked, then shredded into thin strips
1/2 small head cabbage (about 1 lb/500 g), sliced into shreds to yield 4 cups
1 large carrot, coarsely grated to yield 2 cups
1/2 cup (20 g) mint leaves
1 small onion, halved and very thinly sliced
4 tablespoons roasted unsalted peanuts, crushed
Sprigs of coriander leaves (cilantro), to garnish
2 tablespoons Crispy Fried Shallots (page 8), to garnish (optional)

Dressing
1 to 2 finger-length chilies, deseeded and minced
3 cloves garlic, minced
1 tablespoon sugar
1 tablespoon rice vinegar or cider vinegar
3 tablespoons freshly squeezed lime or lemon juice
3 tablespoons fish sauce
3 tablespoons oil
1/4 teaspoon freshly ground black pepper

1 Combine the shredded chicken, cabbage, carrot, mint leaves and onion in a large serving bowl. Set aside.
2 Mix the Dressing ingredients in a bowl until the sugar is dissolved, then pour the Dressing over the vegetables and toss until well combined.
3 Top the salad with the crushed peanuts and garnish with coriander leaves (cilantro) and Crispy Fried Shallots (if using). Serve immediately.

Serves 4 to 6
Preparation time: **20 mins**
Cooking time: **15 mins**

Grilled Leaf-wrapped Beef Rolls

1 lb (500 g) ground beef
24 large wild betel leaves (see note) or grape leaves, soaked in water to soften and drained
8 bamboo skewers, soaked in water for 1 hour before using
1 tablespoon oil
1 portion Fish Sauce Dip (page 8)

Marinade
2 cloves garlic, minced
2 tablespoons minced lemongrass (from the inner part of the thick end of the stalk)
2 shallots, minced
1 teaspoon curry powder
1 teaspoon oyster sauce
2 teaspoons fish sauce
1 tablespoon cornstarch
2 teaspoons sugar
$1/4$ teaspoon salt
$1/2$ teaspoon freshly ground black pepper

1 Combine the Marinade ingredients in a bowl and mix well. Pour the Marinade over the ground beef and mix until well blended. Cover with a cloth and allow to marinate in the refrigerator for at least 2 hours.
2 Prepare the Fish Sauce Dip by following the recipe on page 8.
3 To make a beef roll, place 1 tablespoon of the beef mixture onto a betel or grape leaf. Fold one end of the leaf over the filling, fold in the sides and roll up tightly, then thread the roll onto a bamboo skewer. Continue to make all the rolls in this manner, threading 3 rolls onto each bamboo skewer as shown.
4 Brush the rolls with a little oil and grill the skewers on a pan grill or under a preheated broiler using medium heat for about 5 minutes on each side, until the leaves are slightly charred.
5 Serve the beef rolls with Fish Sauce Dip.

Wild betel leaves are known as la lot *in Vietnam,* daun kaduk *in Malaysia and Indonesia, and* chaa phluu *in Thailand. If you can't find them, use grape leaves instead.*

Makes 8 skewers
Preparation time: 30 mins + 2 hours to marinate
Cooking time: 10 mins

Place the beef mixture onto a betel leaf and fold one end of the leaf over it.

Fold in the sides of the leaf and roll up tightly to form a neat roll.

Tangy Shrimp Salad with Carrot, Cucumber and Mint Leaves

A cheery salad with contrasting colors of orange, green, white and pink, this is a low-calorie dish suitable for hot-weather eating. As part of a whole meal, this serves 6, but for a main dish, plan on serving only 2 to 3 people.

2 small carrots, thinly sliced to yield 2 cups
3 baby cucumbers, thinly sliced
1 spring onion, minced
20 mint leaves
2 tablespoons coarsely chopped coriander leaves (cilantro)
10 oz (300 g) fresh medium shrimp, poached until just cooked, peeled and deveined
2 tablespoons roasted unsalted peanuts, crushed

Dressing
1 finger-length chili, deseeded and sliced
1 tablespoon rice vinegar or 2 teaspoons cider vinegar
2 tablespoons freshly squeezed lime juice
2 tablespoons fish sauce
2 tablespoons oil
2 shallots, thinly sliced
1 teaspoon sugar
$1/4$ teaspoon freshly ground black pepper

1 Combine the carrots, cucumbers, spring onion, mint leaves, coriander leaves (cilantro) and shrimp in a mixing bowl, and set aside.
2 Mix the Dressing ingredients in a bowl until well combined, then pour the Dressing over the vegetables and shrimp, and toss to mix well.
3 Transfer the salad to a serving platter and sprinkle the peanuts on top. Serve immediately.

Serves 4 to 6
Preparation time: **20 mins**

Pork and Shrimp Crepes (Bahn Xeo)

A crepe is a thin pancake with a savory or sweet filling that is popular in French cuisine. The way to eat this Vietnamese crepe is to cut it into small portions and wrap each portion in a lettuce leaf with fresh herbs.

1 cup (125 g) rice flour
1 cup (250 ml) water
1 cup (250 ml) thick coconut milk
$^1/_2$ teaspoon salt
$^1/_4$ teaspoon ground turmeric
1 to 2 tablespoon oil
3 cups (5 oz/150 g) bean sprouts, seed coats and tails removed
2 spring onions, minced
4 oz (120 g) fresh mushrooms, stems discarded, caps thinly sliced to yield about 1 cup
1 portion Fish Sauce Dip (page 8)

Filling
7 oz (200 g) pork, very thinly sliced
8 oz (250 g) fresh medium shrimp, peeled and deveined
4 cloves garlic, minced
1 tablespoon fish sauce
$^1/_2$ teaspoon sugar
2 tablespoons oil
1 onion, halved and sliced

Lettuce Wraps
20 butter lettuce leaves, rinsed and trimmed
Sprigs of mint leaves
Sprigs of coriander leaves (cilantro)
1 cucumber, peeled and thinly sliced

1 Prepare the Fish Sauce Dip by following the recipe on page 8.
2 Make the Filling by combining the pork, shrimp, garlic, fish sauce and sugar in a large bowl and mixing well. Heat the oil in a wok or skillet over medium heat and stir-fry the onion slices for 1 to 2 minutes until fragrant and translucent. Add the pork and shrimp mixture, and stir-fry until the shrimp turn pink, 2 to 3 minutes. Remove and set aside.
3 To make the pancakes, mix the rice flour, water, coconut milk, salt and turmeric in a mixing bowl until a smooth batter is obtained. Set aside for 10 minutes, then strain to remove any lumps.
4 Heat a little oil in a non-stick skillet over medium heat, turning to grease the side. When the pan is hot, pour in $^1/_3$ cup (85 ml) of the batter and turn the pan to obtain a thin round layer of batter, about 8 in (20 cm) in diameter. Scatter a handful of the bean sprouts, spring onion and mushrooms onto the crepe, followed by 2 heaping tablespoons of the Filling on one half of the crepe. Reduce the heat to low, cover the pan and continue to fry for 3 to 4 minutes, until the crepe turns golden brown and crispy. Fold the crepe in half and slide it onto a plate. Repeat until all the batter and Filling are used up.
5 Slice the crepes into sections and arrange with the Lettuce Wraps on a large serving platter. Serve immediately with a bowl of Fish Sauce Dip on the side.

Wrap each section of the crepe in a lettuce leaf together with some mint, coriander leaves (cilantro) and cucumber, and dip in the Fish Sauce Dip.

Makes 5 to 6 crepes or serve 4 to 6
Preparation time: **30 mins**
Cooking time: **40 mins**

Barbecued Lemongrass Beef

This one-dish salad has the advantage of being both delectable and easy to make. You can prepare and assemble everything ahead of time, making this a perfect company meal. Partially freezing the beef firms it and makes for easier slicing. If you wish, you can substitute chicken breast for the beef.

1 lb (500 g) beef sirloin, flank steak or top round, sliced into thin strips
12 bamboo skewers, soaked in water for 1 hour before using
1 tablespoon oil, for brushing
7 oz (200 g) dried rice vermicelli, blanched for 1 to 2 minutes until soft, then rinse with cold water and drained
$1/2$ head lettuce, leaves washed and separated

1 medium cucumber, deseeded and cut into matchsticks
2 cups ($3^1/_2$ oz/100 g) bean sprouts, seed coats and tails removed
Sprigs of mint leaves
Sprigs of coriander leaves (cilantro)
1 small carrot, cut into matchsticks
$1/2$ cup (50 g) roasted unsalted peanuts, crushed
1 portion Fish Sauce Dip (page 8)

Marinade
1 medium onion, sliced
3 cloves garlic
2 stalks lemongrass, thick bottom part only, outer layers discarded, inner part sliced
1 teaspoon salt
$1/2$ teaspoon freshly ground black pepper
$1/2$ teaspoon curry powder (optional)
1 tablespoon fish sauce

1 Make the Marinade first by grinding the onion, garlic and lemongrass to a smooth paste in a blender. Add all the other ingredients and mix until well blended. Transfer the Marinade to a large bowl, place the beef in the Marinade and mix until well coated. Allow to marinate for 1 hour.

2 Prepare the Fish Sauce Dip by following the recipe on page 8.

3 Thread the marinated beef strips onto the bamboo skewers and brush with a little oil, then grill on a pan grill or under a preheated broiler, basting with the Marinade, until just cooked, 2 to 3 minutes on each side.

4 To serve, place the rice vermicelli into individual serving bowls and top with the grilled beef, lettuce leaves, cucumber, bean sprouts, mint leaves, coriander leaves (cilantro) and carrot. Sprinkle with crushed peanuts and serve immediately with a bowl of Fish Sauce Dip on the side.

Dress and toss this dish well with 2 tablespoons of Fish Sauce Dip before eating it.

Serves 6
Preparation time: **45 mins + 1 hour to marinate**
Cooking time: **15 mins**

Vietnamese Pork Pate

This is basically a pork meat loaf, seasoned with fish sauce, black pepper, a touch of sugar and cinnamon. You can enjoy it with French bread and pickles, or served with rice and other dishes.

$1^1/_2$ lbs (700 g) lean pork leg or shoulder, thinly sliced
$^1/_4$ teaspoon ground cinnamon
3 oz (75 g) pork fat, poached for 10 minutes, drained and minced

Marinade
1 tablespoon tapioca flour or cornstarch
3 tablespoons fish sauce
1 teaspoon sugar
1 teaspoon baking soda
$^1/_4$ teaspoon salt
$^1/_4$ teaspoon freshly ground black pepper

Serves 4
Preparation time: 15 mins
+ 6 hours to marinate
  and 15 mins chilling
Cooking time: 1 hour

1 Combine the Marinade ingredients in a large bowl and mix well. Add the pork slices and mix thoroughly with your hands for about 1 minute, until the Marinade is absorbed. Cover the bowl with a cloth and refrigerate for 4 to 6 hours, or overnight if possible, then chill in the freezer for 15 minutes.

2 Preheat the oven to 350°F (180°C).

3 Grind the marinated pork with the cinnamon powder to a smooth paste in a blender. Add the pork fat and pulse several times to mix well.

4 Place the ground pork mixture in a greased loaf pan, smoothing the surface with the back of a moistened spoon, then bake in the oven until cooked, about 1 hour. Remove and set aside to cool.

5 When the pate is cool enough to handle, remove from the pan and cut into slices. Serve with French bread and pickles, or as part of a meal with rice.

Rice Paper Rolls with Marinated Fish and Fresh Herbs (Goi Ca)

Really fresh fish is first "cooked" in vinegar, then combined with onion, herbs, peanuts and fried shallots, and wrapped in rice paper for a light and refreshing starter.

1 cup (250 ml) rice vinegar or cider vinegar
1 lb (500 g) fresh white fish fillets, cut into thick slices
1 tablespoon sugar
1 teaspoon salt
1 onion, very thinly sliced
1 tablespoon minced mint leaves
1 tablespoon minced polygonum leaves (*rau ram* or *laksa* leaves)
1 finger-length red chili, deseeded and minced
2 tablespoons roasted unsalted peanuts, crushed
1 tablespoon Crispy Fried Shallots (page 8)
12 dried rice paper wrappers (each 8 in/20 cm in diameter)
1 ripe starfruit (see note), thinly sliced, to garnish

1 Pour the vinegar over the fish slices and mix well. Allow to marinate at room temperature for 1 hour.
2 After about 30 minutes, rub the sugar and salt into the onion in a bowl, and allow to marinate for 30 minutes.
3 Drain the marinated fish slices and briefly rinse with cold water, then pat dry with paper towels.
4 Squeeze the marinated onion to remove the moisture, then combine with the fish slices, mint, polygonum, chili, peanuts and Crispy Fried Shallots, and mix well. Divide the mixture into 12 equal portions.
5 To make a roll, briefly dip a rice paper wrapper in a bowl of water until soft. Remove and place on a dry surface, smoothing it with your fingers. Place 1 portion of the mixture along one side of the wrapper. Fold the closest edge of the wrapper over the mixture, then fold in the sides and roll up tightly, pressing to seal. Repeat with all the other portions to make a total of 12 rolls.
6 Arrange the rolls on a serving platter, garnish with starfruit or apple slices and serve immediately.

Starfruit is eaten raw and has a tart taste. In some parts of the world, it is known as carambola. If you cannot find it, substitute crisp green apple slices.

Makes 12 rolls or serves 4 to 6
Preparation time: **20 mins + 1 hour to marinate**

Crabmeat Omelete

A versatile and easy dish, this omelete is also very tasty with a filling of cooked ground or minced pork instead of crab. You may also add cut-up ripe tomatoes.

3 tablespoons oil
3 shallots, minced
1 cup (4 oz/120 g) cooked crabmeat
4 eggs, beaten
2 teaspoons fish sauce
1 spring onion, sliced
$1/4$ teaspoon freshly ground black pepper
Sprigs of coriander leaves (cilantro), to garnish

Serves 2 to 4
Preparation time: **5 mins**
Cooking time: **10 mins**

1 Heat 1 tablespoon of the oil in a wok or skillet over medium heat. Stir-fry the shallots for 1 to 2 minutes until fragrant and translucent, then add the crabmeat, mix well and transfer to a mixing bowl.

2 Add the eggs, fish sauce, spring onion and black pepper to the crabmeat mixture and mix well.

3 Heat the remaining oil in the same wok or skillet over medium heat. When the pan is hot, add the egg mixture and cook for 2 to 3 minutes, until crispy and light brown. Flip the omelete over and pan-fry the other side in the same manner. Carefully remove the omelete from the pan with a wide spatula.

4 Place the omelete on a serving platter, garnish with coriander leaves (cilantro) and serve immediately.

Glass Noodle Soup

6 cups (1¹/₂ liters) chicken stock or 2 to 3 stock cubes dissolved in 6 cups (1¹/₂ liters) hot water

Small handful (15 g) dried wood ear fungus, soaked in water until soft, sliced

1 chicken breast (about 4 oz/120 g), poached until done, then shredded along the grain

2 tablespoons fish sauce

¹/₂ teaspoon freshly ground black pepper

¹/₂ teaspoon salt

4 oz (120 g) dried glass noodles, cut into thirds

Sprigs of coriander leaves (cilantro), to garnish

1 Bring the chicken stock and wood ear fungus to a boil over high heat in a pot. Add the chicken and bring the soup to a boil again. Reduce the heat to medium and simmer uncovered for 5 to 10 minutes, seasoning with the fish sauce, black pepper and salt. Add the glass noodles, simmer for 1 to 2 minutes and remove from the heat.

2 Serve hot in individual serving bowls, garnished with coriander leaves (cilantro).

You may substitute lily buds for wood ear fungus, as shown in the photo. Blanch 20 dried lily buds until soft, discard the hard ends and tie each into a knot, then bring the lily buds and chicken stock to a boil in the same manner.

Serves 4
Preparation time: **10 mins**
Cooking time: **20 mins**

Hanoi Beef Noodle Soup (Pho Bo)

This may well be considered Vietnam's national dish. The Vietnamese eat it at any time of the day, but it is especially popular as a breakfast food. What makes this soup so convenient is that you can cook it ahead of time, storing the stock in one container and the remaining ingredients in another.

10 oz (300 g) dried rice stick noodles or rice vermicelli
3 tablespoons fish sauce
1 lb (500 g) beef sirloin or flank steak, cut into very thin slices
2 medium onions, thinly sliced
4 cups (7 oz/200 g) bean sprouts, seed coats and tails removed, blanched until cooked
2 to 3 finger-length chilies, deseeded and sliced
Ground white pepper

Sprigs of coriander leaves (cilantro), to garnish
Sprigs of basil or mint, to garnish
2 lemons or limes, cut into sections, to serve
1 portion Fish Sauce Dip (page 8)

Broth
2 medium onions, peeled and bruised
2 in (5 cm) fresh ginger root, peeled and bruised
3 shallots

10 cups (2^1/$_2$ liters) beef stock or 4 to 5 stock cubes dissolved in 10 cups (2^1/$_2$ liters) hot water
1 lb (500 g) beef shank or brisket
2 star anise pods
1 cinnamon stick
1 teaspoon crushed peppercorns
1 tablespoon salt

Serves 6 to 8
Preparation time: 30 mins
Cooking time: 1^1/$_4$ hours

1 Prepare the Broth first by browning the onions, shallots and ginger under a broiler for 5 to 10 minutes, turning several times, or dry-frying them in a skillet over low heat until slightly burnt on all sides. Remove and transfer to a stockpot. Add all the other Broth ingredients and bring to a boil over medium heat, skimming off the foam and fat that float to the surface. Reduce the heat to low and simmer for 1 hour, until the beef is tender.
2 Prepare the Fish Sauce Dip by following the recipe on page 8.
3 Bring a pot of water to a boil over medium heat. Add the dried noodles and blanch until soft, about 5 minutes for rice stick noodles or 2 minutes for rice vermicelli. Remove and rinse with cold water, then drain.
4 Remove the beef from the Broth and set aside to cool. Strain the Broth to remove all the solids and return the clear Broth to the pot. Season with the fish sauce and keep the Broth hot over very low heat. Slice the beef into thin slices and set aside.
5 To serve, place the rice noodles into individual serving bowls and top with the cooked and raw beef slices, onion slices, bean sprouts and chilies. Ladle the hot Broth into each bowl (the raw beef will partially cook in the boiling soup), sprinkle with pepper and garnish with coriander (cilantro) and basil or mint leaves. Serve hot with lemon or lime sections, and dipping bowls of Fish Sauce Dip on the side.

Creamy Asparagus and Crabmeat Soup

The Vietnamese call asparagus (introduced by the French) "Western bamboo", and transform it into this excellent soup. This soup is normally served on its own, before rice and other dishes, and is good as a starter for any type of meal.

8 oz (250 g) young asparagus spears
4 cups (1 liter) chicken stock or 1 to 2 chicken stock cubes dissolved in 4 cups (1 liter) hot water
1 teaspoon oil
1 clove garlic, minced
2 shallots or the white part of 2 spring onions, minced
1 tablespoon fish sauce
$1/_2$ teaspoon sugar
$1/_2$ cup (2 oz/60 g) cooked crabmeat
2 tablespoons cornstarch, dissolved in 3 tablespoons water
$1/_2$ teaspoon salt
1 teaspoon freshly ground black pepper
1 egg, beaten
2 tablespoons coarsely minced coriander leaves (cilantro) or spring onion greens, to garnish

1 Cut off the bottom one-third of the asparagus spears. Reserve the top parts of the asparagus for later use and cut the bottom parts into short lengths. Bring the chicken stock and the bottom parts of the asparagus to a boil over high heat, then cover and simmer for 15 minutes. Remove from the heat. Strain the stock using a fine sieve and discard the asparagus ends.
2 Cut the reserved top parts of the asparagus into short lengths and set aside.
3 Heat the oil in a wok or saucepan over medium heat and stir-fry the garlic and shallots for 1 to 2 minutes until fragrant and golden brown. Add the clear stock, increase the heat to high and bring the mixture to a boil, seasoning with the fish sauce and sugar. Add the asparagus and simmer uncovered for about 1 minute, until just cooked, then add the crabmeat and mix well.
4 Reduce the heat to medium, pour in the cornstarch mixture, stirring constantly, until the soup is slightly thickened. Season the soup with the salt and black pepper, then pour in the egg in a slow stream, stirring gently until it sets. Remove from the heat.
5 Transfer the soup to a large soup tureen or individual soup bowls and serve hot, garnished with coriander leaves (cilantro) or spring onion greens.

Serves 4
Preparation time: **15 mins**
Cooking time: **30 mins**

Chicken Noodle Soup (Pho Ga)

Traditionally, this meal-in-a-bowl noodle soup is made with beef, but the Vietnamese have also perfected a lighter version using chicken. This soup is popular at any time of day or night, and is often enjoyed for breakfast in Vietnam.

10 oz (300 g) dried rice stick noodles or rice vermicelli
4 cups (7 oz/200 g) bean sprouts, seed coats and tails removed, blanched until cooked
1 onion, thinly sliced
Ground white pepper
1 bunch coriander leaves (cilantro), sliced
1 bunch basil or mint leaves
1 lime, cut into sections, to serve
2 finger-length chilies, deseeded and sliced, placed in a dipping bowl with soy sauce

Broth
10 cups ($2^1/_2$ liters) chicken stock or 4 to 5 stock cubes dissolved in 10 cups ($2^1/_2$ liters) water
$^1/_2$ fresh chicken (about 1 lb/500 g)
1 cinnamon stick
4 spring onions, cut into lengths
1 in ($2^1/_2$ cm) fresh ginger root, peeled and bruised
2 teaspoons sugar
1 teaspoon salt
2 tablespoons fish sauce

1 Prepare the Broth first by bringing the chicken stock, chicken, cinnamon, spring onions, ginger, sugar and salt to a boil over high heat in a stockpot. Reduce the heat to low and simmer for 45 minutes, skimming off the foam and fat that float to the surface. Stir in the fish sauce and remove from the heat. Remove the chicken and set aside to cool. Strain the solids from the Broth using a fine sieve and keep the clear Broth warm over very low heat.

2 Bring a pot of water to a boil over medium heat. Add the dried noodles and blanch until soft, about 5 minutes for rice stick noodles or 2 minutes for rice vermicelli. Remove and rinse with cold water, then drain.

3 When the chicken is cool enough to handle, shred the meat along the grain into thin strips.

4 Place the noodles in individual serving bowls and top with the bean sprouts, shredded chicken and onion slices. Pour the hot Broth into each bowl, sprinkle with pepper and garnish with coriander (cilantro) and basil leaves. Serve hot with the lime and bowls of chilies and soy sauce on the side.

Serves 4 to 6
Preparation time: **20 mins**
Cooking time: **1 hour**

Pineapple Seafood Soup (Canh Chua Tom)

This substantial soup, which has a sweet and sour tang—thanks to the use of pineapple, tamarind juice and tomato—can be made either with shrimp or fish. Serve it with rice and other dishes rather than as a separate course.

1 lb (500 g) fresh seafood (a combination of shrimp, squid and fish fillets), cleaned and shelled, and cut into bite-sized pieces
2 teaspoons oil
$1/2$ onion, thinly sliced
3 stalks lemongrass, thick bottom part only, outer layers discarded, inner part sliced
6 cups ($1^1/2$ liters) chicken or fish stock, or 2 to 3 stock cubes dissolved in 6 cups ($1^1/2$ liters) hot water
1 large ripe tomato, cut into wedges
1 cup (5 oz/150 g) fresh or canned pineapple, cut into chunks
1 tablespoon fish sauce
2 tablespoons tamarind juice (page 7)
1 tablespoon sugar
$1/2$ teaspoon salt
2 cups ($3^1/2$ oz/100 g) bean sprouts, seed coats and tails removed
1 baby cucumber, cut into matchsticks
20 mint leaves or sprigs of coriander leaves (cilantro)

Marinade
2 cloves garlic, minced
1 finger-length red chili, deseeded and minced
1 tablespoon fish sauce
$1/4$ teaspoon freshly ground black pepper

1 Combine the Marinade ingredients in a large bowl and mix well. Place the seafood in the Marinade and mix until well coated. Cover with a cloth and allow to marinate for at least 20 minutes.

2 Heat the oil in a wok or stockpot over medium heat and stir-fry the onion and lemongrass for 1 to 2 minutes until fragrant and tender. Add the chicken or fish stock, tomato and pineapple, mix well and season with the fish sauce, tamarind juice, sugar and salt. Increase the heat to high and bring the mixture to a boil, then simmer uncovered for 1 minute. Add the marinated seafood and simmer for 2 to 3 minutes, until the shrimp turn pink or are just cooked. Finally add the bean sprouts and mix well, adjusting the seasoning by adding more fish sauce and tamarind juice if needed. Remove from the heat.

3 Serve hot in individual serving bowls, topped with cucumber and mint or coriander (cilantro) leaves.

Serves 4 to 6
Preparation time: **15 mins + 20 mins to marinate**
Cooking time: **15 mins**

Cabbage Roll Soup

This elegant recipe consists of cabbage leaves filled with a mixture of pork and shrimp seasoned with fish sauce, pepper and five spice powder, then simmered in chicken stock. The rolls can be prepared in advance and refrigerated until you are ready to cook the soup.

16 cabbage leaves, blanched in boiling water for 1 to 2 minutes until soft, then drained, for wrapping
16 spring onion greens, blanched in boiling water for 10 seconds until soft, then drained
6 cups (1^1/$_2$ liters) chicken stock or 2 to 3 stock cubes dissolved in 6 cups (1^1/$_2$ liters) hot water
1 tablespoon fish sauce
1 portion Fish Sauce Dip (page 8)

Filling
8 oz (250 g) ground pork
8 oz (250 g) fresh medium shrimp, peeled and deveined
16 spring onion bulbs
3 tablespoons sliced coriander leaves (cilantro)
2 teaspoons fish sauce
^{1}/$_2$ teaspoon salt
^{1}/$_2$ teaspoon freshly ground black pepper
^{1}/$_4$ teaspoon five spice powder

1 Prepare the Fish Sauce Dip by following the recipe on page 8.
2 Prepare the Filling by grinding all the ingredients to a smooth paste in a blender. Set aside.
3 To make each cabbage roll, place 1 heaping tablespoon of the Filling along one edge of a blanched cabbage leaf. Fold the leaf over the Filling, then fold in the sides and roll up tightly. Tie the roll securely with a blanched spring onion green. Repeat with the remaining ingredients to make a total of 16 rolls.
4 Bring the chicken stock and fish sauce to a boil over high heat in a stockpot. Add the cabbage rolls and return to a boil. Reduce the heat to medium, cover and simmer for 5 to10 minutes until cooked. Remove from the heat.
5 Serve hot in individual serving bowls with a bowl of Fish Sauce Dip on the side.

Makes 16 rolls or serves 4 to 6
Preparation time: 25 mins
Cooking time: 15 mins

Beef Soup with Lemongrass

Rich beef stock is given a distinctive Vietnamese flavor with lemongrass, ginger and a touch of fish sauce. Paper-thin slices of fresh beef and tomato are added; this tasty soup makes a satisfying meal served together with rice.

7 oz (200 g) beef sirloin or rump steak
2 teaspoons minced garlic
2 teaspoons fish sauce
$^1/_4$ teaspoon freshly ground black pepper
2 spring onions, white bulbs and green leaves separated, both finely sliced
1 teaspoon oil
1 stalk lemongrass, thick bottom part only, outer layers discarded, inner part thinly sliced
2 thin slices fresh ginger root, bruised
6 cups (1$^1/_2$ liters) beef stock or 2 to 3 stock cubes dissolved in 6 cups (1$^1/_2$ liters) hot water
2 teaspoons rice vinegar
1 teaspoon sugar
1 medium tomato, cut into wedges
Sprigs of coriander leaves (cilantro), to garnish

1 Wrap the beef in plastic and chill in the freezer for 30 minutes, then unwrap and cut into paper thin slices. Add 1 teaspoon of the garlic, 1 teaspoon of the fish sauce and the black pepper to the beef and mix well. Set aside to marinate.
2 Heat the oil in a stockpot over medium heat and stir-fry the remaining garlic, spring onion white bulbs, lemongrass and ginger for about 2 minutes until soft. Add the remaining fish sauce, beef stock, rice vinegar, sugar and tomato, and bring to a boil. Reduce the heat to low, cover and simmer for about 5 minutes.
3 Just before serving, bring the soup to a boil again. Add the beef and simmer until just cooked, about 1 minute. Remove and transfer to individual serving bowls. Garnish with spring onion greens and coriander leaves (cilantro), and serve hot.

Serves 4
Preparation time: **15 mins + 30 mins chilling**
Cooking time: **8 mins**

Fried Fish with Lemongrass

Zesty lemongrass cooked with garlic and fresh chilies makes an appetizing complement to freshly-fried fish.

1 $^1/_2$ lbs (700 g) fresh whole fish of fillets, such as red snapper or sea bass
5 tablespoons oil
Sprigs of coriander leaves (cilantro), to garnish

Marinade
2 stalks lemongrass, thick bottom part only, outer layers discarded, inner part minced
3 cloves garlic, minced
2 finger-length chilies, deseeded and minced
2 tablespoons fish sauce
1 teaspoon sugar
$^1/_4$ teaspoon freshly ground black pepper
$^1/_2$ teaspoon curry or turmeric powder

1 If using whole fish, clean and scale the fish and score each side diagonally several times. Pat the fish dry with paper towels and set aside.
2 Combine the Marinade ingredients in a bowl and mix well. Pour the Marinade over the fish and coat the fish evenly. Allow to marinate for at least 1 hour.
3 Heat the oil in a wok or large skillet over medium heat until hot. Pan-fry the marinated fish for about 7 minutes on each side, until crispy and golden brown. Remove and drain on paper towels. Transfer to a serving platter, garnish with coriander leaves (cilantro) and serve immediately.

Serves 4 to 6
Preparation time: 15 mins + 1 hour to marinate
Cooking time: 15 mins

Fish Sauteed with Dill and Tomatoes

This Vietnamese fried fish sings with complementary flavors and textures, and rates high marks. This recipe will serve four as part of a larger meal, but two will finish it without any problems.

1 1/2 lbs (700 g) fish fillets or fish steaks
1 tablespoon fish sauce
1/2 teaspoon freshly ground black pepper
3 tablespoons flour, for dredging
4 tablespoons oil

Sauce
1 tablespoon oil
3 shallots, thinly sliced
4 cloves garlic, minced
3 large ripe tomatoes, blanched, skinned and deseeded, flesh diced (or use 1 cup canned chopped tomatoes)
1/2 cup (125 ml) chicken stock or 1/4 stock cube dissolved in 1/2 cup (125 ml) hot water
1 1/2 tablespoons fish sauce
1 teaspoon sugar
1 spring onion, cut into short lengths
1/4 cup (10 g) minced dill
2 tablespoons minced coriander leaves (cilantro)
4 tablespoons roasted unsalted peanuts, crushed (optional)

1 Place the fish fillets or steaks on a plate. Rub the fish sauce and black pepper into the fish, then dredge the fish in the flour until thoroughly coated. Shake off the excess flour.

2 Heat the oil in a wok or large skillet over medium heat until hot. Pan-fry the coated fish until golden brown, 4 to 5 minutes on each side. Remove from the heat and drain on paper towels. Set aside.

3 To make the Sauce, heat the oil in a wok or skillet over medium heat and stir-fry the shallots and garlic until fragrant and golden brown, 1 to 2 minutes. Add the tomatoes and stir-fry for 2 more minutes. Add the chicken stock and simmer uncovered for about 5 minutes, seasoning with the fish sauce and sugar. Finally add the fried fish, spring onion, dill and coriander leaves (cilantro), and mix well. Remove from the heat and transfer to a serving platter. Sprinkle the peanuts (if using) on top and serve hot with steamed rice.

Serves 4
Preparation time: **20 mins**
Cooking time: **20 mins**

Fish in Caramel Sauce

The Vietnamese typically use catfish for this dish, but any firm-fleshed fish will do. Use whole fish or large slices of cross-cut fillets as these keep whole better. The fish is delicious served over steamed rice.

2 tablespoons oil
1$^1/_2$ lbs (700 g) catfish fillets, cut into thick slices
$^1/_2$ in (1 cm) fresh ginger root, peeled and grated
Sprigs of coriander leaves (cilantro), to garnish

Caramel Sauce
$^2/_3$ cup (135 g) sugar
$^1/_2$ cup (125 ml) fish sauce
8 shallots, thinly sliced
$^1/_2$ teaspoon freshly ground black pepper

1 To make the Caramel Sauce, heat the sugar in a skillet over low heat, stirring constantly, until it begins to melt and caramelize, after 3 to 5 minutes. Remove from the heat and add the fish sauce. Return the pan to the heat and bring the mixture to a boil over medium heat. Simmer uncovered for about 5 minutes, stirring constantly until the mixture turns into a thick syrup. Add the shallots and black pepper, mix well and remove from the heat. This yields about $^2/_3$ cup (165 ml) of sauce.
2 Heat the oil in a wok or skillet over medium heat. Add the fish and stir-fry for 2 to 3 minutes. Add the ginger and Caramel Sauce, and bring the mixture to a boil. Reduce the heat to low and simmer uncovered for 5 more minutes, until the fish is cooked. Remove from the heat and transfer to a serving platter.
3 Garnish with coriander leaves (cilantro) and serve hot with steamed rice.

Serves 4 to 6
Preparation time: **10 mins**
Cooking time: **10 mins**

Stir-fried Fish with Mushrooms and Ginger

The perfect duo, fresh ginger and bean sauce, perk up this stir-fried fish. For the snappiest flavor, look for fresh young ginger.

3 tablespoons oil
3 cloves garlic, minced
3 in (8 cm) fresh ginger root, peeled and cut into thin strips to yield 1/2 cup
3 fresh shiitake mushrooms, stems discarded, caps sliced into thin strips
1 tablespoon *hoisin* sauce
1/4 cup (60 ml) chicken stock or 1/8 stock cube dissolved in 1/4 cup (60 ml) hot water
1 lb (500 g) flounder or other white fish fillets, thinly sliced
2 teaspoons fish sauce
1 teaspoon sugar
1/2 teaspoon freshly ground black pepper
1 to 2 finger-length chilies, deseeded and cut into thin strips (optional)
1 spring onion, cut into lengths, to garnish
Sprig of coriander leaves (cilantro), to garnish

1 Heat the oil in a wok or skillet over medium heat. Stir-fry the garlic, ginger and mushrooms for 2 to 3 minutes, until fragrant. Add the *hoisin* sauce and stir-fry for a few seconds, then add the chicken stock and bring the mixture to a boil. Stir in the fish pieces and simmer uncovered, seasoning with the fish sauce, sugar and black pepper, until cooked, 3 to 5 minutes. Finally add the chili (if using), mix well and remove from the heat.

2 Transfer to a serving platter, garnish with spring onion and coriander leaves (cilantro), and serve hot with steamed rice.

Serves 4
Preparation time: **8 mins**
Cooking time: **10 mins**

Honey Ginger Shrimp

In this easy recipe, large shrimp are marinated then stir-fried, with honey added at the last minute for a delicious touch of sweetness. For a more dramatic appearance, peel the shrimp but leave the heads and tails intact.

1$^1/_2$ lbs (700 g) fresh large shrimp, peeled and deveined
2 tablespoons oil
3 cloves garlic, minced
1 tablespoon soy sauce
1$^1/_2$ tablespoons honey
2 spring onions, cut into lengths

Marinade
$^1/_2$ tablespoon rice wine, sherry or sake
2 teaspoons fish sauce
1 tablespoon ginger juice (pressed from grated young ginger root)
1 teaspoon freshly ground black pepper

1 Combine the Marinade ingredients in a large bowl and mix well. Place the shrimp in the Marinade and mix until well coated. Allow to marinate for at least 30 minutes.
2 Heat the oil in a wok or large skillet over high heat and stir-fry the garlic until fragrant and golden brown, about 30 seconds. Add the shrimp and the Marinade, and stir-fry until the shrimp turn pink and are just cooked, about 1 minute. Season with the soy sauce and honey, and continue to stir-fry for 2 more minutes. Finally add the spring onions and mix well. Remove from the heat, transfer to a serving platter and serve hot with steamed rice.

Serves 4
Preparation time: **10 mins + 30 mins to marinate**
Cooking time: **5 mins**

Stir-fried Garlic Shrimp

1½ lbs (700 g) fresh
  large shrimp, peeled
  and deveined
3 tablespoons oil
4 cloves garlic, minced
1 to 2 finger-length
  chilies, deseeded and
  minced
1 tablespoon oyster
  sauce
Sprigs of coriander leaves
  (cilantro), to garnish

Marinade
2 teaspoons minced garlic
1 tablespoon fish sauce
¼ teaspoon salt

1 Combine the Marinade ingredients in a large bowl and mix well. Place the shrimp in the Marinade and mix until well coated. Allow to marinate for at least 30 minutes.
2 Heat the oil in a wok or large skillet over high heat, add the shrimp and stir-fry until cooked, 2 to 3 minutes. Remove from the heat and transfer to a serving platter.
3 Reheat the remaining oil in the pan over medium heat. Stir-fry the garlic and chilies for 1 to 2 minutes, until fragrant, and season with the oyster sauce. Remove from the pan and spoon the mixture over the shrimp. Garnish with coriander leaves (cilantro) and serve hot with steamed rice.

Serves 4
Preparation time: 10 mins + 30 mins to marinate
Cooking time: 7 mins

Black Pepper Sauce Crabs

2 to 3 fresh medium
  crabs (3 lbs/1$^1/_2$ kg)
3 tablespoons oil
1 tablespoon minced garlic
1 tablespoon freshly
  ground black pepper
$^1/_2$ teaspoon sugar
$^1/_2$ teaspoon salt
$^1/_2$ cup (125 ml) chicken
  stock or $^1/_4$ stock cube
  dissolved in $^1/_2$ cup
  (125 ml) hot water
1 spring onion, thinly
  sliced

Serves 4
Preparation time: **20 mins**
Cooking time: **15 mins**

1 Scrub and rinse the crabs thoroughly. Detach the claws from each crab. Lift off the carapace and discard. Scrape out any roe and discard the gills. Rinse well, halve the crabs with a cleaver and crack the claws with a mallet.
2 Heat the oil in a wok over high heat and stir-fry the garlic and black pepper until fragrant, about 30 seconds. Add the crabs and stir-fry for 2 to 3 minutes, seasoning with the sugar and salt. Add the chicken stock, mix well and simmer for 3 to 5 minutes, covering the wok. Finally add the spring onion, stir well and remove from the heat.
3 Transfer the crabs to a serving platter and serve immediately.

Spicy Lemongrass Shrimp

This easy shrimp dish has a touch of sweetness typical of many Vietnamese dishes, as well as the fragrance of lemongrass, rice wine and fish sauce. Stir-fry over high heat for the best flavor and texture.

1¹/₂ lbs (700 g) fresh medium shrimp, peeled and deveined
2 tablespoons oil
2 teaspoons minced garlic
¹/₄ teaspoon salt
Sprigs of coriander leaves (cilantro), to garnish

Marinade
2 teaspoons fish sauce
2 teaspoons rice wine, sherry or sake
2 teaspoons sugar
1 finger-length red chili, deseeded and minced or ground to a paste in a mortar
¹/₄ teaspoon freshly ground black pepper
1 stalk lemongrass, thick bottom part only, outer layers discarded, inner part thinly sliced
1 teaspoon minced garlic

1 Combine the Marinade ingredients in a large bowl and mix well. Place the shrimp in the Marinade and mix until well coated. Allow to marinate for at least 30 minutes.

2 Heat the oil in a wok over high heat and stir-fry the garlic until fragrant and golden brown, about 30 seconds. Add the shrimp with the Marinade, and stir-fry until the shrimp turn pink and are just cooked, 2 to 3 minutes. Finally season with the salt and remove from the heat.

3 Transfer to a serving platter, garnish with coriander leaves (cilantro) and serve hot with steamed rice.

Serves 4
Preparation time: **20 mins + 30 mins to marinate**
Cooking time: **5 mins**

Stuffed Crabs

This recipe for crabs stuffed with crabmeat, pork and seasonings is really delicious, and as it can be prepared well in advance, it's ideal for entertaining. For a quicker and an easier version, use cooked crabmeat instead of fresh crabs and form the Filling into crab cakes to be pan-fried.

Oil for deep-frying
Sprigs of coriander leaves
  (cilantro), to garnish

Filling
4 fresh medium crabs
  (about 1 lb/500 g each)
4 oz (120 g) ground pork
3 shallots, minced
1 clove garlic, minced
2 to 3 shiitake mush-
  rooms, stems discarded,
  caps minced
1 small packet (25 g)
  dried glass noodles,
  soaked in water until
  soft and drained, cut
  into short lengths to
  yield $1/2$ cup
1 egg, beaten
2 teaspoons fish sauce
$1/2$ teaspoon freshly
  ground black pepper
2 teaspoons cornstarch,
  for dredging

Serves 4 to 6
Preparation time: **25 mins**
Cooking time: **30 mins**

1 To make the Filling, scrub and rinse the crabs thoroughly, then steam for 20 to 25 minutes, until cooked. Set aside to cool. Detach the claws from each crab and lift off the carapace. Reserve the carapace to be stuffed later, discard the gills and spongy grey matter from each crab, then quarter the crab with a cleaver and crack the claws with a mallet. Carefully extract the crabmeat from all the crabs and claws, and place in a large bowl. Combine the crabmeat with all the other ingredients and mix well. Divide the crabmeat mixture into 4 equal portions.

2 Pat the carapaces dry with paper towels. Dredge the inside of each carapace with $1/2$ teaspoon of the cornstarch, shaking off the excess cornstarch. Wet your hands, stuff each carapace with a portion of the crabmeat mixture. The stuffed crabs can now be refrigerated until just before they are required.

3 Heat the oil in a wok or saucepan over medium-high heat until hot. Gently lower the stuffed crabs into the hot oil, with the stuffed side facing down, and deep-fry for 2 to 3 minutes on each side, until crispy and golden brown. Remove and drain on paper towels.

4 Arrange the stuffed crabs on a serving platter, garnish with coriander leaves (cilantro) and serve.

Alternatively, you can make crab cakes by using 12 oz (350 g) cooked crabmeat in place of the fresh crabs. Combine the crabmeat with all the other ingredients and mix well. Flour your hands, form the Filling into little patties (each from $1^1/2$ tablespoons of the Filling), then deep-fry for 2 to 3 minutes over medium heat until crispy and golden brown.

Honey Ginger Chicken

Delicately flavored with ginger and garlic, accented with a touch of five spice powder, fish sauce, soy sauce and black pepper, this stir-fried chicken dish is glazed to a succulent sweetness with honey.

3 tablespoons oil
1 large onion, cut into wedges
1 lb (500 g) boneless chicken thighs, thinly sliced
1 tablespoon minced garlic
2 in (5 cm) fresh ginger root, peeled and cut into very thin strips
$^1/_2$ teaspoon five spice powder
1 tablespoon fish sauce
2 tablespoons soy sauce
2 tablespoons honey
$^1/_2$ teaspoon freshly ground black pepper
1 finger-length red chili, deseeded and cut into thin strips, to garnish

1 Heat the oil in a wok or skillet over high heat until very hot. Stir-fry the onion until fragrant and translucent, 30 seconds to 1 minute. Add the chicken and stir-fry for 1 to 2 minutes. Add the garlic and ginger, and stir-fry for another 30 seconds. Reduce the heat to medium, add the five spice powder and mix well. Season with the fish sauce, soy sauce and honey, and stir-fry for 2 more minutes until the chicken is cooked and well coated with the sauce. Remove from the heat and transfer to a serving platter.
2 Sprinkle the black pepper on top and garnish with chili. Serve hot with steamed rice.

Serves 4
Preparation time: 10 mins
Cooking time: 8 mins

Spicy Lemongrass Tamarind Chicken

1 lb (500 g) boneless chicken thighs, sliced into bite-sized pieces
2 tablespoons oil
3 cloves garlic, minced
1 finger-length red chili, deseeded, then cubed
1 small bell pepper, deseeded, then cubed
$^1/_2$ cup (125 ml) chicken stock or $^1/_4$ chicken stock cube dissolved in $^1/_2$ cup (125 ml) hot water
2 tablespoons tamarind juice (page 7)
1 tablespoon sugar
Sprigs of coriander leaves (cilantro), to garnish

Marinade
$1^1/_2$ tablespoons fish sauce
1 tablespoon sugar
2 teaspoons dried chili flakes or 1 teaspoon ground red pepper
$^1/_4$ teaspoon freshly ground black pepper
1 stalk lemongrass, thick bottom part only, outer layers discarded, inner part thinly sliced

1 Combine the Marinade ingredients in a large bowl and mix well. Place the chicken pieces in the Marinade and mix until well coated. Cover with a cloth and allow to marinate for at least 30 minutes.
2 Heat the oil in a wok or skillet over medium heat, stir-fry the garlic for 1 to 2 minutes until fragrant and golden brown. Add the chicken, chili and bell pepper, increase the heat to high and stir-fry until the chicken is browned, about 2 minutes. Reduce the heat to medium, add the chicken stock, tamarind juice and sugar, and bring the mixture to a boil. Simmer uncovered for about 3 minutes, stirring occasionally, until the chicken is tender and cooked. Remove from the heat.
3 Transfer to a serving platter, garnish with coriander leaves (cilantro) and serve with steamed rice.

Serves 4
Preparation time: 15 mins + 30 mins to marinate
Cooking time: 8 mins

Chicken and Sweet Potato Coconut Curry

This enjoyable combination of chicken and sweet potato with a touch of curry powder and creamy coconut milk is an easily made, mild yet flavorful dish which will appeal to those who do not like highly spiced food.

1 fresh chicken (about 3 lbs/1 1/2 kg), cut into bite-sized pieces
Oil for deep-frying
3 sweet potatoes (about 1 lb/500 g), peeled and cubed, dried with paper towels
1 tablespoon minced garlic
1 large onion, quartered, layers separated
3 bay leaves
2 stalks lemongrass, thick bottom part only, outer layers discarded, inner part cut into lengths
1 carrot, cubed
2 cups (500 ml) water
1 cup (250 ml) thick coconut milk

Marinade
2 to 3 tablespoons curry powder
1 teaspoon sugar
1 teaspoon salt
1/4 teaspoon freshly ground black pepper

1 Combine the Marinade ingredients in a large bowl and mix well. For a milder flavor, use less curry powder. Place the chicken pieces in the Marinade and mix until well coated. Cover the bowl with a cloth and allow to marinate for at least 1 hour.

2 Heat the oil in a wok over medium heat until very hot. Deep-fry the sweet potatoes, in several batches, until crispy and golden brown, 2 to 3 minutes. Remove with a slotted spoon and drain on paper towels.

3 Drain off all but 1 tablespoon of the oil in the wok. Reheat the oil over high heat and stir-fry the garlic until fragrant and golden brown, about 30 seconds. Add the onion, bay leaves and lemongrass, and stir-fry for 1 minute, until tender. Add the marinated chicken pieces and stir-fry until the color changes, 2 to 3 minutes, then add the carrot and water, and bring the mixture to a boil. Cover and simmer for about 15 minutes, stirring occasionally, until the chicken is cooked through. Finally add the sweet potatoes and coconut milk, mix well and simmer uncovered for 10 to 15 minutes. Remove from the heat.

4 Transfer the curry to a serving platter and serve with steamed rice or crusty French bread.

Serves 4 to 6
Preparation time: **25 mins + 1 hour to marinate**
Cooking time: **45 min**

Ginger and Five Spice Fried Chicken

In Vietnam, quail—such tiny birds that two are needed per person— are used for this dish. However, chickens marinated in a mixture of seasonings and honey, then steamed and deep-fried, make an ideal substitute.

1 fresh chicken (about 3 lbs/1 $^1/_2$ kg), cut into 8 pieces
Oil for deep-frying
Sprigs of coriander leaves (cilantro), to garnish

Marinade
$^1/_4$ cup (50 g) crushed rock sugar or 4 tablespoons sugar
4 shallots, sliced
2 in (5 cm) fresh ginger root, peeled and sliced
4 cloves garlic
$^1/_2$ cup (125 ml) water
$^1/_4$ cup (60 ml) soy sauce
2 tablespoons rice wine, sherry or sake
2 teaspoons five spice powder
$^1/_2$ teaspoon freshly ground black pepper

Serves 4
Preparation time: 15 mins
 + 2 hours marinating
Cooking time: 35 mins

1 Make the Marinade first by grinding the sugar, shallots, ginger and garlic to a smooth paste in a blender. Transfer to a small saucepan, combine with all the other ingredients and mix well. Bring the Marinade to a boil over medium heat, then simmer uncovered, stirring regularly, until the sugar is dissolved. Remove from the heat, transfer to a large bowl and set aside to cool.
2 Place the chicken in the Marinade and mix until well coated. Cover with a cloth and allow to marinate in the refrigerator for at least 2 hours, basting the chicken pieces with the Marinade several times.
3 Drain off the Marinade and steam the marinated chicken for about 25 minutes in a steamer. Remove from the steamer and set aside to cool for at least 30 minutes.
4 Pat the chicken dry with paper towels. Heat the oil in a wok over high heat until very hot, and deep-fry the chicken, a few pieces at a time, until crispy and golden brown, 2 to 3 minutes on each side. Remove from the pan and drain on paper towels.
5 Serve hot, garnished with coriander leaves (cilantro).

You may keep the chicken whole for a better presentation, as shown in the photo. Use more oil to deep-fry the whole chicken. If keeping to the same amount of oil, baste the chicken regularly with the hot oil while deep-frying.

Caramel Chicken Wings

Vietnamese love the salty-sweet taste of food cooked in caramel sauce, and often use the sauce to enliven shrimp, fish, pork and chicken. These tasty wings will be the hit of any meal and are ideal partners for a mild-tasting vegetable dish.

2$^1/_4$ lbs (1 kg) fresh chicken wings, cut into bite-sized pieces
1 teaspoon grated fresh ginger root
1 portion Caramel Sauce (page 53)

Serves 4 to 6
Preparation time: **10 mins**
Cooking time: **35 mins**

Bring all the ingredients to a boil over high heat in a large saucepan. Reduce the heat to low, cover and simmer for about 30 minutes, stirring occasionally, until the chicken is cooked. Remove from the heat, drain off any fat and serve immediately.

Grilled Lemongrass Spareribs

2¹/₄ lbs (1 kg) spareribs, cut into separate ribs

Marinade
2 stalks lemongrass, thick bottom part only, outer layers discarded, inner part sliced
3 shallots
4 cloves garlic
1 finger-length red chili, deseeded
¹/₂ portion Caramel Sauce (page 53)

Serves 4 to 6
Preparation time: **15 mins**
 + 1 hour to marinate
Cooking time: **30 mins**

1 Prepare the Marinade first by grinding the lemongrass, shallots, garlic and chili to a smooth paste in a blender. Combine with the Caramel Sauce and mix well. Pour the Marinade over the ribs, spread evenly with your fingers until the ribs are well coated. Allow to marinate for at least 1 hour.

2 Preheat the oven to 350°F (180°C). Bake the marinated ribs in the Marinade for about 20 minutes in the oven, turning over once, then turn on the broiler and grill the ribs for an additional 5 minutes on each side, basting with the Marinade, until well browned. Remove from the heat, transfer to a serving platter and serve immediately.

Stuffed Tomatoes

In this Vietnamese version of French *tomates farcies*, tomatoes are stuffed with a savory mixture of minced pork and Chinese mushrooms. The tomatoes can be filled and the sauce partially prepared in advance, reducing the time needed during the final stages of preparation.

4 large ripe tomatoes
2 tablespoons oil
Sprigs of coriander
    leaves, to garnish

Filling
7 oz (200 g) ground pork
2 large dried black
    Chinese mushrooms,
    soaked in hot water until
    soft, stems discarded,
    caps minced
2 cloves garlic, minced
2 shallots, minced
1 spring onion, minced
2 teaspoons fish sauce
$1/_2$ teaspoon sugar
$1/_4$ teaspoon freshly
    ground black pepper

Sauce
2 ablespoons water
$1/_2$ tablespoon fish sauce
$1/_2$ tablespoon oyster
    sauce
1 tablespoon sugar
2 cloves garlic, minced

Serves 4
Preparation time: 30 mins
    + 20 mins to marinate
Cooking time: 25 mins

1 Make the Filling first by combining all the ingredients in a bowl and mixing well. Set aside for at least 20 minutes, then divide into 4 equal portions.
2 Using a sharp knife, carefully slice off about ($1/_2$ in) 1 cm of the top of each tomato, then scoop out the pulp to form the tomato cups. Reserve the pulp for the Sauce and place the cups inverted on a plate to drain off all the liquid.
3 To make the Sauce, mince the reserved tomato pulp and bring it to a boil over medium heat in a small saucepan, then simmer uncovered for about 10 minutes. Remove from the heat and set aside to cool. Press the cooked pulp through a sieve into a bowl, and mix with the water, fish sauce, oyster sauce and sugar until well combined.
4 Dry the inside of each tomato cup with a paper towel. Fill each cup with a portion of the Filling. Heat the oil in a wok or skillet over medium heat, pan-fry the stuffed tomatoes, with the opened end facing down first, for 3 to 5 minutes. Turn the stuffed tomatoes right side up and pan-fry the bottoms for another 3 to 5 minutes, until cooked. Remove from the pan and transfer to a serving dish.
5 Reheat the remaining oil in the pan over medium heat and stir-fry the garlic for 1 to 2 minutes, until fragrant and golden brown. Add the prepared Sauce, mix well and bring to a boil, then simmer uncovered for about 2 minutes, stirring occasionally. Remove from the heat and pour the sauce over the stuffed tomatoes. Garnish with coriander leaves and serve hot with steamed rice.

Sesame Beef with Bamboo Shoots

3 tablespoons oil
12 oz (350 g) beef sir-
  loin, thinly sliced
3 cloves garlic, minced
3 spring onions, cut into
  lengths
8 oz (250 g) canned or
  pre-packed frozen bam-
  boo shoots, drained
  and thinly sliced
1 tablespoon fish sauce
1 tablespoon oyster sauce
$1/_4$ teaspoon salt
$1/_4$ teaspoon freshly
  ground black pepper
4 tablespoons sesame
  seeds, dry-roasted in a
  skillet for 10 minutes
  over low heat until
  browned

1 Heat 2 tablespoons of the oil in a wok or skillet over high heat. Stir-fry the beef for about 1 minute, until it changes color. Remove from the heat and set aside.
2 Heat the remaining oil in the wok or skillet, stir-fry the garlic, spring onions and bamboo shoots for 2 to 3 minutes, seasoning with the fish sauce, oyster sauce, salt and pepper. Return the beef to the pan, add the sesame seeds and stir-fry for 3 more minutes, until the beef is tender and cooked. Remove from the heat.
3 Transfer to a serving platter and serve hot with steamed rice.

Serves 4
Preparation time: **10 mins**
Cooking time: **10 mins**

Barbequed Pork Skewers

1 lb (500 g) streaky pork, cubed
16 bamboo skewers, soaked in water for 1 hour before using
1 small cucumber, thinly sliced, to garnish

Marinade
1 tablespoon honey
1 tablespoon *hoisin* sauce
1 tablespoon fish sauce
3 cloves garlic, minced
2 spring onions, minced
2 teaspoons oyster sauce
$1/_2$ teaspoon salt
$1/_2$ teaspoon freshly ground black pepper

1 Combine the Marinade ingredients in a large bowl and mix well. Place the pork in the Marinade and mix until well coated. Cover the bowl with a cloth and allow to marinate for at least 1 hour.

2 Thread the pork onto the bamboo skewers and grill, a few skewers at a time, on a pan grill or under a pre-heated broiler using medium heat for 2 to 3 minutes on each side, turning and basting frequently with the Marinade, until cooked. Alternatively, grill in the oven for 5 minutes on each side.

3 Arrange the grilled pork on a serving platter, garnish with sliced cucumber and serve immediately.

Makes 16 skewers
Preparation time: **20 mins + 1 hour to marinate**
Cooking time: **8 mins**

Hearty Beef Stew with Vegetables

This dish always wins much praise, and may become your favorite way to serve beef stew. This works well served with rice, pasta or French bread.

$1^1/_2$ lbs (700 g) beef, cubed
2 tablespoons oil
1 large onion, diced
4 cloves garlic
3 cups (750 ml) water
4 tablespoons tomato paste
2 star anise pods
1 large carrot, cut into chunks
2 medium potatoes, cut into chunks
1 small daikon radish (about 12 oz/350 g), peeled and cut into chunks to yield about 2 cups

Marinade
2 stalks lemongrass, thick bottom part only, outer layers discarded, inner part minced
1 finger-length red chili, deseeded and diced
2 tablespoons minced fresh ginger root
1 teaspoon ground cinnamon
1 teaspoon curry powder
2 tablespoons fish sauce
1 teaspoon salt
$1/_4$ teaspoon freshly ground black pepper

1 Make the Marinade first by combining all the ingredients in a large bowl and mixing well. Place the beef cubes in the Marinade and mix until well coated. Allow to marinate for at least 30 minutes.
2 Heat the oil in a wok or large saucepan over high heat and stir fry the onion and garlic until fragrant, 30 seconds to 1 minute. Add the marinated beef and the Marinade and stir-fry for about 3 minutes, until the beef is browned on all sides. Add the water, tomato paste and star anise, and bring the mixture to a boil. Reduce the heat to low and simmer uncovered for about 1 hour. Add the vegetables and continue to simmer for another 20 minutes, until the beef is tender and the vegetables are cooked. Remove from the heat, transfer to a serving bowl and serve with steamed rice.

Serves 6 to 8
Preparation time: **20 mins + 30 mins to marinate**
Cooking time: **1 hour 25 mins**

Grilled Meatballs with Peanut Sauce

These meatballs are equally good grilled over charcoal or broiled under an oven grill.

1 lb (500 g) lean pork or beef, sliced
2 cloves garlic minced
1 tablespoon rice wine, sherry or sake
$1/_2$ teaspoon sugar
$1/_2$ teaspoon salt
1 tablespoon Roasted Rice Powder (page 8)
1 tablespoon fish sauce
1 tablespoon oil
12 bamboo skewers, soaked in water for 1 hour before using
1 portion Peanut Dipping Sauce (page 8)

Accompaniments
4 oz (120 g) dried rice vermicelli, blanched for 1 to 2 minutes until soft, then rinsed with cold water and drained
1 to 2 heads butter lettuce, leaves washed and separated
1 cup (40 g) mint leaves
1 bunch coriander leaves (cilantro)
1 medium cucumber, deseeded and cut into thin strips
$1/_2$ small ripe pineapple, peeled and cubed

1 Make the meatballs first by combining the pork or beef, garlic, rice wine, sugar and salt in a large bowl, and mixing until well blended. Allow to marinate for at least 30 minutes.

2 While the meat is marinating, make the Peanut Dipping Sauce by following the recipe on page 8.

3 Grind the marinated mixture in a food processor, then combine in a bowl with the Roasted Rice Powder (page 8), fish sauce and oil, and mix well. Wet your hands, spoon 1 heaping tablespoon of the meat mixture and shape it into a ball. Repeat until all the meat mixture is used up. Thread the meatballs onto the bamboo skewers and grill, a few skewers at a time, on a pan grill or under a preheated broiler using medium heat for about 5 minutes each, turning frequently, until evenly browned and cooked through.

4 Arrange the meatballs with the Accompaniments on a serving platter and serve with bowls of Peanut Dipping Sauce on the side.

Invite your guests to wrap the meatball in a lettuce leaf together with small amounts of all the other Accompaniments before eating it.

Makes 36 meatballs
Preparation time: **30 mins + 30 mins to marinate**
Cooking time: **20 mins**

Caramelized Pork

This beautifully simple pork dish is full of flavor. Although it is normally made with streaked belly pork, you can use a leaner cut such as shoulder if you prefer. This dish reheats well and can be made well in advance.

1 lb (500 g) belly or shoulder pork, cut into thick slices
1 tablespoon oil
1 tablespoon sugar
1 1/2 cups (375 ml) unsweetened coconut water (see note)
Sprigs of coriander leaves (cilantro), to garnish

Marinade
3 shallots, minced
2 cloves garlic, minced
1 tablespoon sugar
1/4 teaspoon freshly ground black pepper
3 tablespoons fish sauce
1 teaspoon soy sauce

Serves 4
Preparation time: **10 mins**
  + 1 hour to marinate
Cooking time: **1 hour**

1 Combine the Marinade ingredients in a bowl and mix until the sugar is dissolved. Pour the Marinade over the pork slices, mix until well coated and allow to marinate for at least 1 hour.

2 Heat the oil in a wok or skillet over medium heat until very hot. Add the marinated pork and stir-fry until the pork begins to brown, 3 to 5 minutes. Add the sugar and continue to stir-fry for 2 to 3 minutes, until the sugar caramelizes and the pork turns dark brown. Finally pour in the coconut water and bring the mixture to a boil. Reduce the heat to low, cover and simmer the mixture for 35 to 45 minutes, stirring occasionally, until the sauce has reduced to half and the pork is tender. Remove from the heat.

3 Transfer to a serving platter, garnish with coriander leaves (cilantro) and serve hot with steamed rice.

Coconut water is NOT the same as coconut milk—it is the clear juice contained inside young coconuts, and is available canned or in packets in speciality shops. If unavailable, substitute water instead.

Stir-fried Beef with Pineapple

When you want something simple and quick to serve with rice, try this beef stir-fried with pineapple, bell pepper and onion.

1 lb (500 g) sirloin or topside steak, thinly sliced across the grain
2 cloves garlic, minced
1 tablespoon fish sauce
$1/2$ teaspoon freshly ground black pepper
3 tablespoons oil
1 large onion, cut into wedges
1 large bell pepper, deseeded and cubed
2 cups (10 oz/300 g) pineapple chunks
1 tablespoon oyster sauce
2 teaspoons sugar
2 teaspoons cornstarch, dissolved in $1/2$ cup (125 ml) beef stock or water

1 Combine the beef slices, garlic, $1/2$ tablespoon of the fish sauce and black pepper in a large bowl, and mix with your fingers until the beef is well coated. Set aside for 10 minutes to marinate.

2 Heat 1 tablespoon of the oil in a wok or skillet over high heat until very hot. Stir-fry the marinated beef until it changes color, about 1 minute. Remove from the pan and set aside.

3 Heat the remaining oil in the wok or skillet over high heat until hot, stir-fry the onion and bell pepper for about 1 minute until tender, then add the pineapple and stir-fry for 1 to 2 more minutes, seasoning with the remaining fish sauce, oyster sauce and sugar. Return the beef to the pan and mix well. Pour in the cornstarch mixture and stir-fry until the sauce is thickened. Remove from the heat.

4 Transfer to a serving platter and serve immediately.

Serves 4 to 6
Preparation time: 15 mins + 10 mins to marinate
Cooking time: 5 mins

Tangy Lemongrass Beef Fondue

When the Vietnamese go out to celebrate, they often order an expensive seven-course meal known as "Beef in Seven Ways". This tangy fondue is always served as the first course, as it really gets the taste buds going.

1 lb (500 g) sirloin steak, in one piece
1 large onion, thinly sliced
2 spring onions, sliced diagonally
1 tablespoon oil
1 teaspoon freshly ground black pepper
1 1/2 portions Fish Sauce Dip (page 8)

Lemongrass Dip
1 tablespoon oil
4 cloves garlic, minced
2 in (5 cm) fresh ginger root, peeled and thinly sliced
3 cups (750 ml) water
3/4 cup (185 ml) white vinegar
1/4 cup (50 g) sugar
1 tablespoon tomato paste
2 stalks lemongrass, thick bottom part only, outer layers discarded, inner part bruised
1 1/2 teaspoons salt

Serves 4
Preparation time: **30 mins + 30 mins chilling**
Cooking time: **15 mins + table-top cooking**

Accompaniments
16 dried rice paper wrappers (each 8 in/20 cm in diameter), dipped briefly in water to soften
16 lettuce leaves
1/2 cup (20 g) mint leaves
1/2 cup (20 g) coriander leaves (cilantro)
1 small cucumber, halved lengthwise, thinly sliced
2 ripe tomatoes, quartered

1 Wrap the beef in plastic and chill in the freezer for 30 minutes until semi-frozen, then unwrap and slice finely across the grain. Arrange the beef slices on a large serving platter, top with some sliced onion and spring onions, and sprinkle with the oil and black pepper. Cover and set aside until required.
2 To make the Lemongrass Dip, heat the oil in a pot or saucepan over medium heat. Stir-fry the garlic and ginger for 1 to 2 minutes until fragrant. Add the remaining ingredients and bring to a boil. Reduce the heat to low, cover and simmer for 10 minutes. Remove from the heat and transfer to a steamboat or fondue pot.
3 To serve, place the Lemongrass Dip in the middle of the dining table and keep the Dip simmering over low heat. Arrange the beef, the remaining onion and spring onions, Accompaniments and dipping bowls of Fish Sauce Dip around the Lemongrass Dip.
4 Invite your guests to dip the beef slices (using chopsticks) briefly in the hot Lemongrass Dip until they have just change color or are just cooked. Remove and wrap the beef slices in a rice paper wrapper with some of the Accompaniments, and dip in the Fish Sauce Dip before eating.

Sweet Glutinous Rice with Coconut and Red Beans

The nutty taste of black glutinous rice and azuki beans is popular throughout Southeast Asia. In this simple Vietnamese version, they are soaked and steamed, then sweetened with sugar and coconut cream, and given a slight crunch with peanuts. Serve as a snack or dessert.

1 cup (200 g) uncooked black glutinous rice, soaked in water overnight to soften, then drained
$1/4$ cup (50 g) dried red azuki beans, soaked in water overnight to soften, then drained
$1/4$ cup (50 g) superfine caster sugar
$1/2$ cup (125 ml) coconut cream
2 tablespoons roasted unsalted peanuts, crushed

1 Combine the glutinous rice and azuki beans in a bowl and mix well.
2 Line a bamboo steamer with a cheesecloth and spread the rice and bean mixture evenly on it. Steam for 20 minutes, then turn the mixture over and steam for 10 more minutes on the other side until cooked.
3 While the cooked rice and bean mixture is still hot, add the sugar and mix until well combined.
4 To serve, divide the sweetened rice and bean mixture in individual serving bowls, top with 1 teaspoon of the crushed peanuts and drizzle with some coconut cream. Serve warm or at room temperature.

Serves 4 for 6
Preparation time: 10 mins + overnight soaking
Cooking time: 40 mins

Ginger-flavored Crème Brulèe

This is a Vietnamese version of the popular French Crème Brulèe, flavored with fresh ginger rather than the traditional vanilla bean. A chilled custard of pure cream is covered with a thin crust of crunchy glazed sugar.

2 cups (500 ml) cream
2$^1/_2$ in (6 cm) fresh ginger root, peeled, then halved and bruised
3 egg yolks
$^1/_4$ cup (50 g) superfine caster sugar
4 ovenproof bowls (each 4 in/10 cm in diameter)
1 large baking dish (which the 4 bowls fit into)
4 tablespoons sugar

Serves 4
Preparation time: **15 mins**
 + 15 mins standing
 + 2 hours chilling
Cooking time: **35 mins**

1 Heat the cream and ginger in a saucepan over low heat, stirring from time to time, until the mixture almost comes to a boil. Remove from the heat, cover the pan and set aside for 15 minutes. Remove and discard the ginger pieces.

2 Preheat the oven to 350°F (180°C).

3 Mix the egg yolks and caster sugar in a large bowl until the sugar is dissolved, then gradually pour in the ginger-flavored cream, whisking to mix well. Do not beat the cream as this will cause air bubbles in the custard.

4 Pour the custard mixture into 4 ovenproof bowls and place them in a deep baking dish. Carefully fill the baking pan with boiling water up to half the height of the bowls, then bake in the oven until the cream just sets in the middle, 30 to 35 minutes. Remove and set aside to cool. When the custard is cool enough, chill in the refrigerator for at least 1 hour.

5 Sprinkle the top of each custard with 1 tablespoon of the sugar and grill under a preheated broiler for about 1 minute, until the sugar blisters and turns golden brown. (Alternatively, you may sear the surface of the custard using a torch.) Remove and set aside to cool.

6 Return the custard to the refrigerator and chill for at least 1 hour before serving.

Coconut Creme Caramel

Vietnamese chefs have adapted some classical French dishes to incorporate local ingredients, as in this version of Creme Caramel where coconut milk is substituted for cream, and cooked with extra milk, eggs and sugar to make a rich custard with a caramel topping.

$^1/_2$ cup (100 g) sugar
$^1/_2$ cup (125 ml) water
6 ovenproof bowls (each about 4 in/8 cm in diameter)
1 cup (250 ml) milk
1 cup (250 ml) thick coconut milk
4 eggs
$^1/_4$ cup (50 g) superfine caster sugar
$^1/_2$ teaspoon vanilla essence
$^1/_4$ cup (25 g) freshly grated coconut
1 large baking dish (which the 4 bowls fit into)

Makes 6
Preparation time: **5 mins** + 1$^1/_2$ **hours chilling**
Cooking time: **45 mins**

1 Bring the sugar and 3 tablespoons of the water to a boil in a small saucepan over medium heat, without stirring. Simmer until golden brown, about 4 minutes, then add the remaining water and return to a boil, stirring. Remove from the heat and pour the caramel syrup equally into 4 ovenproof bowls. Set aside.
2 Heat the milk and coconut milk in a saucepan over medium heat until just warm. Remove and set aside.
3 Whisk the eggs, caster sugar and vanilla essence in a large bowl until the sugar is dissolved. Gradually add the warm milk mixture, a little at a time, and whisk to mix well. Strain the mixture into a large jug and stir in the grated coconut.
4 Preheat the oven to 325°C (160°C).
5 Pour the mixture equally into the bowls containing the caramel syrup. Place the bowls in a baking dish half-filled with boiling water and bake in the oven until set, 30 to 40 minutes. Remove from the oven and set aside to cool, then chill in the refrigerator.
6 Serve the chilled caramel in the bowls or inverted onto serving platters.

Bananas in Coconut Milk

This super-fast dessert is delicious served hot or cold.

1 cup (250 ml) water
2 cups (500 ml) thick coconut milk
1 pandanus leaf, washed and tied into a knot, or few
    drops pandanus or vanilla essence (optional)
$^1/_2$ cup (100 g) sugar
$^1/_4$ teaspoon salt (optional)
3 tablespoons sago pearls (see note), rinsed and
    drained
6 small or 3 large ripe bananas, peeled, halved length-
    wise, then cut into thick slices
$^1/_4$ cup (30 g) sesame seeds, dry-roasted in a skillet for
    10 minutes over low heat until browned

1 Heat the water, coconut milk, pandanus leaf or
essence, sugar and salt in a large saucepan over medium heat, stirring constantly, until the sugar is dissolved. Reduce the heat to low, add the sago pearls,
cover and simmer over low heat for 5 to 7 minutes,
stirring from time to time, until the sago pearls are half
cooked. Add the bananas and simmer uncovered for
another 5 to 7 minutes, stirring from time to time,
until the sago pearls turn translucent. Remove from
the heat.
2 Serve cold or hot in individual serving bowls with a
sprinkling of sesame seeds on top.

Sago pearls are tiny white balls made from the starch
of the sago palm. They soften and turn transparent
when cooked, and help thicken coconut milk or water
with their gluey texture. Sago pearls are available in
packets in the dry foods section of Asian supermarkets.

Serves 4 to 6
Preparation time: **15 mins**
Cooking time: **10 mins**

Complete Recipe Listing

Bananas in Coconut
Milk 94

Barbecued Lemongrass
Beef 28

Barbecued Pork Skewers 77

Beef Soup with
Lemongrass 47

Black Pepper Sauce
Crabs 59

Cabbage Roll Soup 45

Caramel Chicken Wings 72

Caramel Sauce 53

Caramelized Pork 83

Chicken and Sweet Potato
Coconut Curry 69

Chicken Noodle Soup (Pho
Ga) 41

Classic Pork and Crabmeat
Spring Rolls 12

Coconut Creme Caramel 93

Crabmeat Omelete 34

Creamy Asparagus and
Crabmeat Soup 38

Crispy Fried Shallots 8

Fish in Caramel Sauce 53

Fish Sauce Dip (Nuoc Cham)
8

Fish Sauteed with Dill and
Tomatoes 51

Fresh Vietnamese Salad
Rolls 15

Fried Fish with Lemongrass
48

Ginger and Five Spice Fried
Chicken 70

Ginger-flavored Crème
Brulèe 90

Glass Noodle Soup 35

Green Papaya Salad 11

Grilled Leaf-wrapped Beef
Rolls 22

Grilled Lemongrass Chicken
Satays 9

Grilled Lemongrass
Spareribs 73

Grilled Meatballs with
Peanut Sauce 81

Hanoi Beef Noodle Soup
(Pho Bo) 36

Hearty Beef Stew with
Vegetables 78

Honey Ginger
Chicken 65

Honey Ginger Shrimp 56

Lemongrass Dip 87

Peanut Dipping Sauce (Nuoc
Leo) 8

Pickled Bean Sprouts and
Carrot 10

Pineapple Seafood Soup
(Canh Chua Tom) 42

Pork and Shrimp Crepe
(Bahn Xeo) 26

Rice Paper Rolls with
Marinated Fish and Fresh
Herbs (Goi Ca) 33

Roasted Rice Powder 8

Seasoned Shrimp on a Sugar
Cane Stick 18

Sesame Beef with Bamboo
Shoots 76

Shredded Chicken and
Cabbage Salad 20

Spicy Lemongrass
Shrimp 60

Spicy Lemongrass Tamarind
Chicken 66

Stir-fried Beef with
Pineapple 84

Stir-fried Garlic Shrimp 58

Stir-fried Fish with
Mushrooms and Ginger 54

Stuffed Crabs 63

Stuffed Tomatoes 74

Sweet Glutinous Rice with
Coconut and Red Beans 89

Tangy Lemongrass Beef
Fondue 87

Tangy Shrimp Salad with
Carrot, Cucumber and
Mint Leaves 25

Vietnamese Pork Pate 30

Vietnamese Seared Beef
Salad 17